Zen Minds

Achieve Happiness, Focus and Peace in Your Everyday Life by Incorporating Principles and Practices of Zen Buddhism

By Matt McKinney

© **Copyright 2019 - All rights reserved.**

The content contained within this book may not be reproduced, duplicated or transmitted without direct written permission from the author or the publisher.

Under no circumstances will any blame or legal responsibility be held against the publisher or author for any damages, reparation, or monetary loss due to the information contained within this book. Either directly or indirectly.

Legal Notice:

This book is copyright protected. This book is only for personal use. You cannot amend, distribute, sell, use, quote or paraphrase any part, or the content within this book, without the consent of the author or publisher.

Disclaimer Notice:

Please note the information contained within this document is for educational and entertainment purposes only. All effort has been executed to present accurate, up to date and reliable, complete information. No warranties of any kind are declared or implied. Readers acknowledge that the author is not engaging in the rendering of legal, financial, medical or professional advice. The content within this book has been derived from various sources. Please consult a licensed professional before attempting any techniques outlined in this book.

By reading this document, the reader agrees that under no

circumstances is the author responsible for any losses, direct or indirect, which are incurred as a result of the use of information contained within this document, including, but not limited to, —errors, omissions, or inaccuracies.

Table of Contents

Introduction 1
Chapter 1: What Does Zen Mean? 2
    The Origins of Zen 3
    What to Do? 4
    What Not to Do? 6
Chapter 2: Remember to Breathe 9
    Breathing for Relaxation 10
    The Benefits 11
    The Complete Yogi Breath 13
    Bellows Breath 14
    Breath Counting 15
Chapter 3: Shift Your Perspective 17
    Stay with One Thing at a Time 18
    Concentrate on the Process 20
    Don't Rationalize 22
Chapter 4: Streamline Your Life 24
    Prioritize 26
    Declutter 27
    Build a Positive Skillset 29
Chapter 5: Be Aware of the Present 31
    Slow Down 32
    Appreciate the Moment 33

Have Fewer Expectations 35

Chapter 6: Don't Forget to Meditate Each Day 37

    Yoga 39

    Qigong 40

    Guided Visualization 42

Chapter 7: You Need a Daily Routine 44

    Eating Well 45

    Exercise 47

    Lower Stress 49

Chapter 8: Know How to Stop and Appreciate Life 51

    Learn To Let Go 52

    Turn More to Nature 54

    Happiness Is Closer Than You Think 55

Conclusion 58

Thank you for purchasing this book and I hope that you will find it beneficial. If you will want to share your thoughts on this book, you can do so by leaving a review on the Amazon page, it helps me out a lot.

Introduction

A Zen lifestyle is an effort to lead a less complex life. To accomplish so successfully, you will need to undertake a series of habits that reduce, streamline and sort out the mayhem of your everyday life.

By integrating Zen habits into your everyday regimen, you can find out how to concentrate on what's significant in life and give all your awareness to that. Simultaneously, you will also hone in your skills to get rid of the unnecessary and unimportant things from life. The aim is to lead a simpler yet more deliberate and successful life.

This book will help you get going with Zen basics and how to implement these habits into your life.

Chapter 1: What Does Zen Mean?

You might not have engaged in it, but you most likely know about Zen. It is a popular word doing the rounds in various circles, mainly where people are seeking a way to simplify their lives.

As a matter of fact, Zen has frequently been related to aspects like serenity, mindfulness, focus and anything else that can serve to help recover some order in today's fast-paced and turbulent lives. Basically, Zen makes an effort to comprehend the meaning of life without being sidetracked by logical or rational thought.

The practice does require a strong discipline which, when adhered to appropriately, will allow you to get better at eluding distractions. But this is simpler said than done. If you originate from the western part of the hemisphere where intellectual thinking and multitasking prevail, it can be demanding to adjust to Zen.

The Origins of Zen

Traditionally, Zen has been performed for centuries in Oriental monasteries by monks and goes by numerous titles. For example, the Chinese describe it as Ch' an, the Vietnamese as Thien and the Koreans as Seon. However, it is the Japanese portrayal of this element of Buddhism that is referred to as Zen.

Zen Buddhism was delivered to China by the Indian monk, Bodhidharma at some point in the 6th century. After that, it came to be known as Ch' an and after that spread to Korea and Japan. Under the sixth Chinese patriarch, Huineng, Zen dropped a lot of its intrinsic Indian trappings ending up being more Chinese. It also ended up being more of the Zen that we currently think of.

However, it was not until the middle of the 20th century that Zen Buddhism came to be well-known in the West.

Zen, as we understand it right now, is a way of living where folks find joy and tranquility inside themselves. They discover how to be more mindful of their environments and the present as opposed to being distracted by an influx of information overload. Zen instructs these people to lead a more disciplined and uncomplicated life rather than a contrived and artificial one.

So if you are looking for a way to incorporate more Zen into your life then read on. Here is a swift review of what to incorporate and what to omit from your life as you start your Zen journey.

What to Do?

At its very basic, Zen instructs you to be completely mindful and live in every moment. This suggests you should operate with a single-pointed awareness.

For example, if you're tidying up, then you're completely present for the process of cleaning alone. If you're hanging out with family, they are your sole focus and nothing else. Or if you're unwinding at home, then you're not contemplating the day's events or stressing over tomorrow.

Keeping things uncomplicated and directed also lets you recognize that less is more. So even though you may be doing less, you're really giving it your all and coming out with a content experience.

Maintaining things minimal will also enable you to identify what's significant and trivial in life. In a way, it's decluttering your day-to-day affairs. But decluttering here doesn't just refer to your tangible life as in handling everyday tasks and chores, but also decluttering your mind.

Many times, you get caught up in contrasting or puzzling thoughts which can truly impact your mood. As such, you end up being sidetracked, absent-minded, and even anxious. This, consequently, shows up in your behavior, potentially making you scared, bothered and preoccupied. You want to rid yourself of all this to live a Zen lifestyle.

Then there is your attachment to your aims and desires. Now, this is not a negative thing provided that you work towards it positively. However, if you reach a moment where you persuade yourself that you can't be joyful without it, at that point you're in trouble.

This sort of attachment is unhealthy. Sadly, lots of people succumb to this attitude. To go into the Zen zone in your life, you have to respond to a few questions first.

Ask yourself why you're working toward your goal. Is it due to the fact that you assume you'll find joy? Or is it something that will allow you to aid others? Maybe, you consider it worthwhile spending your time on?

Now look on the other side and notice what this quest is costing you in regards to your personal wellbeing or the wellbeing of others. If you are convincing yourself that you'll be satisfied when you attain your goal, that in itself is hindering you from appreciating the moment.

Anything that prevents you from living in the present also keeps you from discovering happiness and calmness in that very same moment.

So to really experience a Zen lifestyle, you have to work both on your body and your mind. On a bodily level, practices such as inhaling and exhaling, smiling more, and meditation can all enable you to control the turmoil in life. But the same can likewise have a remarkably serene impact on your mind.

If the disorder in your tangible life is brought down, then your state of mind will also loosen up.

What Not to Do?

Just like it's essential to understand what steps to follow when embracing a Zen lifestyle, it's just as vital to understand what not to do as well.

You need to discover peace with yourself initially before you can move onto anything else. And to accomplish that you have to be pleased with who you are. In short, you can say that you need to get to like yourself more to start with. In which way do you accomplish that?

For starters, you need to quit comparing yourself or your circumstance to others. When you compare, you undermine your joy and start to feel lacking. Damaging thoughts like what you possess or don't begin to creep up and you make yourself agonize for no reason. You want to end that immediately.

That said, you likewise need to quit judging. Judging certainly never feels good due to the fact that judgment is a weighty burden.

An additional thing you may wish to work on is worry. If you wish to embrace Zen habits for a better, more relaxed lifestyle, you should reduce stressing over everything. Oftentimes, worry originates from fear or an impulse to feel in control. In the event that you feel that you're beginning to lose control, you start to worry.

This is precisely what doesn't work in a Zen lifestyle. Worrying simply produces harmful energy within yourself and close to you. And with a distressed head on your shoulders, you won't have the ability to concentrate on the present.

The do's and don'ts of Zen are a mishmash. Some are simple and fast, while others are more of a work-in-progress. But over time, if you adhere to these steps regularly, they will converge and change your life in a major way.

Chapter 2: Remember to Breathe

You can call this a concrete and psychological aspect of Zen habits. While the practice on its own may be bodily in nature, it does have really amazing psychological benefits.

Bodily, because it consists of the innate actions of breathing in and breathing out. And psychological because your mind and your breathing pace are always connected. Just consider it, a fast, out-of-control breath leads to a fast, out-of-control mind or the other way around.

In moments of mental stress, your nervous system overcomes you. This results in a surge in heart rate and tense muscles. Your breathing ends up being fast and this impacts your body on the whole.

Even so, very few people understand the healing qualities that breathing has. Your breath could be utilized to take care of these fluctuations. This, consequently, leads to muscle relaxation and less stress on the nervous system.

Meanwhile, when your breathing is at peace and composed, so is your mind. Here is how composed breathing can enable you to attain a Zen life.

Breathing for Relaxation

Have you ever tried taking a truly deep breath? Give it a go and you will feel more relaxed and less nervous immediately.

You have no idea how valuable your breath is. Turning breathing exercises into the aspect of your life can produce considerable progress not just in your quality of breath, but likewise the quality of life. You will feel enhanced vibrancy and purity that you may have been losing out on for quite a while.

When performing breathing, choose calm breathing. Calm breathing generally entails breathing gradually and is very useful. It decreases bodily symptoms, like panic attacks and anxiety. This is a procedure that could be practiced anyplace, whenever. Using this technique, when you breathe to unwind you really instruct yourself on how to do stress management.

And the significance of a cool and composed mind in Zen habits can not be underestimated. Even folks who don't have a Zen lifestyle have been discovering how to manage their breath for a long period of time. That's due to the fact that it has long been a technique of soothing the brain in yoga and meditation. And currently, it's even being utilized to subdue anxiety and to restrain panic attacks in clinical and psychiatric practices.

Basically, controlled breathing enables you to clear the head and body of negativity. The same also turns on the mind and spirit. Ancient yogis have devoted years applying and fine-tuning ideal breathing techniques. To them, breathing is the simplest and most organic way to discharge stress.

The Benefits

Breathing for comfort has enormous benefits. There are numerous on a bodily level like detoxing. In fact, whenever you inhale, your body possibly releases about 70% of toxins.

Appropriate exhalation discharges optimal carbon dioxide, which likewise clears the body of toxins. As this continuous state of cleansing occurs, your head also clears out, and you feel a whole lot better.

In a different area, breathing serves as a masseuse for your organs. The stomach, liver, pancreas all get massage therapy when you take a breath. The constant motions of the diaphragm and abdomen throughout breathing permits circulation to improve greatly, and studies explain that breathing aids in strengthening muscles.

Appropriate oxygen amount also helps in reducing the strain on the heart. When you take a breath correctly, you make your lungs proficient. The lungs begin acquiring more oxygen which is good for the heart. This decreases strain on the heart to provide oxygen to the cells.

On its advantages for the mind, correct breathing helps in reducing stress, loosens up the mind and can even boost your mood.

You understand that the moment you're in a state of rage, your body stiffens and tenses and your breathing ends up being shallow. As this takes place, the supply of oxygen to the body declines. However, understanding to breathe properly enables the oxygen to arrive at all areas of the body effectively.

Similarly, breathing correctly has even been linked to lowering the formation of clots. When you breathe actively, you enable tightened areas to soften. Whenever this takes place, you have the ability to bring clarity as the body is loosened up.

You are likewise mindful that when the mind rests, you feel less mental. With a content mindset, there is a feeling of power that the body goes beyond. By doing this, breathing serves to help reduce emotional strain and the anxious feelings that accompany it.

A lot of these impacts of conscious breathing will make your Zen lifestyle additionally powerful. You know already that when your mind finds yourself in a peaceful state, your body will react likewise. So here are a couple of techniques to unwind your body and mind.

The Complete Yogi Breath

The concept behind this method is to fill your whole abdomen and chest with air. Clean air should get in your body like a new spirit and reinvigorate it. This interior process likewise extends your spine, sculpts internal organs, and enhances circulation across the body.

To accomplish this, breathe out entirely so that everything hollows out. After a brief pause, breathe in deeply. As you breathe in feel your tummy expand outward. Afterward, move your attention to your lower back and edges, filling them with oxygen.

As soon as you've filled these with oxygen, move your attention to your ribcage occupying the midsection of your abdomen. Permit your ribs to bulge.

Ultimately, fill your upper chest area completely to your collarbones. This ought to also elevate your heart as you assume a tall posture. This whole inhalation may be performed in a few brief seconds or spread out to a prolonged period of 15 or so seconds.

For the exhalation, keep your chest raised and your posture high. Beginning with the tummy first, breathe out and clear the belly. Then move toward your spine and clear the midsection. Finish off the exhalation with clearing the chest. Preferably, your exhalation ought to be lengthier than your inhalation or at the very least of identical length.

Bellows Breath

Influenced by yoga and other meditation approaches, this approach can help boost awareness, clear up your mind and make you lively. If you feel sluggish, fuzzy, or as if you're moving in snail's pace, have a go at this breathing technique.

Sitting up high, loosen up your shoulders and take a couple of deep breaths in and out via your nose. Commence the bellows breath by breathing out using your nose. Follow by breathing in via the nose once more. This technique should make sure that your breath originates from your diaphragm.

As you do all this, ensure to maintain your head, neck, shoulders and chest completely still. Complete one routine of 10 breaths followed by a 15-30 second breather. Begin the following round with 20 breaths.

Take a break and after that carry out the last round of 30 bellows breaths. This method is most effectively performed first thing in the morning when you want to start your day properly. You can additionally do this throughout your mid-day slump or just prior to a workout session.

Breath Counting

This is a straightforward technique utilized in Zen practices to soothe an engaged mind.

Begin with abdominal inhales and exhales. By the end of the initial exhalation, create a mental note stating "one." Breathe in, breathe out and mentally state "two." Carry on inhaling and exhaling until you get to "ten." Next begin counting in reverse until you get to "one."

The point here is to keep an eye on the numbers so that your focus remains and doesn't depreciate. This workout is a strength-building one for the mind. It eliminates sidetracking thoughts and grows concentration power. So in case you've never given much consideration to your respiration, now's the opportunity to begin.

Chapter 3: Shift Your Perspective

Frequently, people sense that their concentration is not under their control. You may have had the same hunches regarding yourself. However, the fact is that what you pay attention to is what you experience. If you devote a lot of time concentrating on things you don't require, your head gets caught in a web.

You attempt to multitask, shift from one thing to the following, or just wind up putting things off. And with time, it ends up being difficult to break away from the habit of shifting and being sidetracked all the time.

Nonetheless, the straightforward truth is that your joy hinges on the way you think and how you react to the surroundings you reside in. Perception has a huge part to play when it pertains to yourjoy. So how do you teach your mind to remain more concentrated, and how can you change your perspective?

Here are some measures you can take to accomplish this.

Stay with One Thing at a Time

A lot of people are guilty of carrying out lots of things simultaneously. When you ask for your attention to jump from one thing to another, you are going to have a hectic, fractured, and probably unsuccessful day.

Shifting tasks often requires a supreme degree of performing, implying that you need to use a ton of brainpower and energy even before you begin an activity. No surprise it winds up draining your effectiveness.

Zen educates you to perform the exact opposite. With Zen habits in your life, you are going to select a task that requires performing and then stay with it. A great starting point might be to question why this specific task is significant for you. In case you can offer yourself a sufficient explanation why this undertaking means more than others, then that's where you really need to begin.

As you start off with your activity, switch all your focus to it. Block out any distractions and clear your mind. Don't consider or start doing something different until you have wrapped up what you started. Teach yourself to concentrate on the task at hand and withstand the impulse to look elsewhere.

This practice will maintain you continuously grounded in the present and enable you to deliver your best to whatever undertaking you decide to do. This rule applies to also the easiest of things. For example, whenever you eat, simply eat. Whenever you pour water, merely perform that. Whenever you go walking, simply walk. In circumstances where you may need to move onto another thing, at the very least put away the incomplete task to go back to later.

Taking it slow in this manner doesn't imply you're careless. What it does indicate is that you're doing it properly. You may be undertaking less, but you're accomplishing it effectively.

In some cases, you'll need to handle everyday distractions, such as the digital world for example. Actually, there is now a great deal of research suggesting the fact that digital diversions are making people not just stupid but also uneasy.

Not just does this concern prevent you from focusing, but it likewise stops you from relaxing, both of which are just as harmful.

Concentrate on the Process

Changing point of view needs your focus. You can't embrace a positive life in case you are continuously sidetracked and losing focus on crucial matters.

Paying attention to the process and how things ought to be handled will make you smarter. It's worth to point out that it's extremely important that rather than paying attention to the outcome, learn to concentrate on the process. This will aid you in numerous various ways.

For example, concentrating on the process will remove external factors. What this implies is that choices founded on outcomes often wind up using the incorrect techniques.

But whenever you concentrate on how to get things accomplished, you are far better equipped to refine your skills. As you work your way through anything, you recognize the mistakes and also uncover ways to remediate the problems.

Plus, concentrating on the process also allows you to appreciate the moment. You become more involved in the here and now and at what you're carrying out. And you are going to accomplish it better too.

Another benefit of concentrating on the process instead of the outcome is that you obtain more control over what you're carrying out. Simply put, you don't possess control over the outcome; however, you do have command over the process.

Whenever you give anything your best, the result is likely to get good too. If anything, concentrating on the process will make you more self-assured in mastering new skills. These skills will make you greater at deciding. You will have less concern about the future, and your concentration will be on the present.

To better concentrate on the process, participate in just one thing at a time. Do the work progressively and intentionally. (This doesn't mean nonchalantly, only that you want to take your time and move actively). When doing this, make your motions intentional instead of haphazard.

There is also a necessity to place room between things. What this suggests is that youattempt not to arrange things too close together but leave a few gaps in between. This will provide you with a more calm framework to work with. It will also offer some wiggle room if one activity takes longer than anticipated. The whole purpose of Zen is to take pleasure in what you're doing, so try not to hurry through your life.

Don't Rationalize

Rationalization is described as something where you supposedly develop rational explanations for particular behaviors. The idea is to make that behavior seem ideal even if it's not. Nevertheless, the same interpretation could likewise lead you to assume that rationalization, basically, is the process of producing excuses. In either case, rationalizing doesn't consistently help, which is the reason why you need to stay away from it.

When you wish to integrate Zen habits into your life, you need to quit making excuses. As you've observed earlier, Zen does necessitate a certain level of discipline. So while skipping one day of meditation won't thwart your progress much, turning it into a habit absolutely can.

The largest problem with skip-days such as these is that they ultimately result in quitting or losing hope. The one-time exception then turns into the rule. Getting off track can render it very hard to return on track. That's the reason why Zen promotes establishing a regular regimen as we will see in the next chapter.

In the meantime, let's discuss a bit more with regards to rationalization. You utilize rationalization when you attempt to support less than ideal behavior or feelings. So what you're accomplishing is locating a way to misshape facts to make things seem better than they really are.

Here's something to consider- you say you're going to stick to a diet plan, but that just lasts the initial three days. Or you plan to go to the gym since you got a membership, but you only make it happen one time.

So what takes place here? A few prospects might be that you aren't serious with regards to it, you fail to remember why it's significant, or it becomes too hard. You may also quit in frustration or you begin to rationalize.

When something ends up being hard, your mind rationalizes informing you it's fine if you miss something once, or it's fine to have just another (considering that you worked so hard for it). Even though this may all appear sensible, it begins to undermine your plans. And once you begin believing these rationalizations, following anything becomes almost impossible.

Chapter 4: Streamline Your Life

The world you inhabit today subjects you to many difficulties. At times you wind up convoluting life because of overthinking. Or else, you find yourself overspending, overworking or perhaps even overcommitting.

Overall, it's an attempt to get a lot of things completed in a small amount of time. Overdoing something also worsens things while Zen attempts to educate you on how to keep life uncomplicated. If you wish to have a joyful life, you need to learn the art of simplification. Returning to its initial philosophy, this simply implies keeping just the significant things part of your life and getting rid of the rest.

If you consider your material belongings, eliminating unnecessary or unused stuff will definitely clear your space. This will certainly give you comfort and make you pleased to have a tidy and open house to reside in. (Try not to pack it in with more unwarranted stuff, for that just destroys the concept of simplification).

But whenever you take the same concept to another level, streamlining life can likewise help you survive dark times. When you free your head of negativity, and disruptive thoughts that don't make a difference, you also give space to your mind. This space will enable you to take in things that are truly significant.

Tidy up your mind by consuming just what keeps it fresh. Assume, if you're a book collector and continue stocking books forever, there will come a moment when you'll run out of room. You'll either have to cease purchasing new books or discard some old ones.

Likewise, if you continue adding needless worry and things to your life there will also arrive a time when you'll cave in. Alternatively, if you decide to pick only what is vital, you'll feel lightweight and healthier. How you wish your life to be depends entirely on your decisions.

Here's another example to think about. Assume you keep hanging on to a grudge and dislike for somebody. Ultimately, you'll only be squandering your time and energy dwelling over potential situations that might never transpire. The sole way you can conquer all this is to streamline your life by releasing things that don't matter.

Prioritize

Once more, let's begin with a reminder of what's essential to you. Make this your unquestionable priority and stay with it.

Preferably, the structure of your day-to-day life should be an image of your priorities. If you claim that family is your priority, then make a decision to spend an appointed time with your partner and children. If you claim health is a priority, then you ought to be doing whatever you can for a healthier you. Are you really steering clear of bad/tempting foods and obtaining your daily amount of exercise? Or are your other obligations interfering with that?

Whenever you prioritize, you need to be truthful with yourself. What do you really want and what is standing in your way? If you are able to answer these two questions truthfully, you can begin streamlining your life fairly quickly.

As you prioritize, you'll likewise be filtering out a bunch of hindrances. Simply put, you'll be unscrambling your life. It can end up being a process where you reorganize so your life so that it strongly mirrors your priorities.

If you want to spend more excellent time with your children and other significant half, then simplify your emails, put down your mobile phone or perhaps cut down on your work hours. If you truly wish to paint, then tidy up your room and create a studio area for yourself. The moment you have prioritized your interests, proceed to the following step.

Declutter

When you consider "declutter," you're considering physical in addition to psychological space.

This is a procedure of removing where you do away with everything that is pointless in life or no more provides a utility. You can begin small by setting aside 15-20 minutes of your day decluttering a selected section of your house. It might be a counter or a closet. Stop after 15 minutes and return to it the following day. Or you might assign one whole morning to clean out your kitchen or wardrobe and get it done.

You can opt for whichever approach benefits you the most. As you clear, designate three boxes identified as "garbage," "keep" and "perhaps. The initial two should be simple enough if you comply with this guidance. Anything that you haven't utilized in the previous year can go. You perhaps won't use it in the following year as well. Keep it in the event that you apply it all the time and it still has some years remaining in it.

The "perhaps" stash could be a tad tricky, but don't allow it bewilder you. This ought to be for items about which you're not quite sure. Keep the box concealed, and if you don't utilize it in the following six months, throw it out too. The trick for effectiveness in decluttering is to be ruthless.

The fewer things you possess, the less interferences there will be, and the easier your life. You'll notice that one of the things that provide you genuine comfort is a well-kept, uncomplicated house. When you deal with decluttering your head, you'll discover that overthinking leaves open your mind to obstruction.

As a result of overload, you are not able to think correctly. You want to handle this promptly as it won't enable you to be joyful for long. A clogged mind becomes uninformed of anything occurring around it. The flow of clutter you've built up will turn your mental area into a disorderly wreck. And soon enough, similar to your wardrobes and your cupboards, your mind needs cleaning up too.

If you're uncertain about what sort of psychological clutter is holding you.back, just contemplate these things:

Stressing over the future

Pondering about the past

Contemplating regular routines

Grievances and grudges

Regrets

Obligations

In case these thoughts are continuously on your mind, you want to clear out some headspace.

For starters, not all things require focus. What's happened before is done and can't be reversed. What the future holds is not completely in your control so move across that bridge when you arrive at it.

Any adverse thoughts that you might be holding need to leave as well for these will regularly hold you down.

Build a Positive Skillset

You need to accomplish more than simply existing; you need to thrive. The majority of people think that existing is sufficient just due to the fact that they have too much happening with insufficient time to get it accomplished. It keeps them so hectic that they can't truly deal with things such as simplification.

The issue with this situation is that they lose out on the substance of life. To streamline means to delight in a little bit of management. Control your time and your life intelligently, so you cultivate a skillset of long-lasting habits.

As you streamline things when beginning or quitting a habit, it can make performance a lot easier. For instance, if you wish to join a gym, select one that is near your home. This will make it easier for you to head there each day conveniently. If you select one that's distant, not only will you waste a great deal of time arriving, you may stop sooner than intended due to the distance.

 Likewise, maintaining things straightforward can also train you to end up being more organized. When you engage in simplification, you discover how to manage things more effectively. This minimizes the aspect of wastefulness and you not only find out how to save on expenses but also how to enhance your general lifestyle standards.

And ultimately, when you convolute things, you also squander a bunch of time. You overthink things that don't necessitate focus and complicate them additionally.

Streamlining such things teaches you punctuality and the value of time. By maintaining things simple, you find out how to get them accomplished properly and on time.

Chapter 5: Be Aware of the Present

Mindfulness is a capability that helps you acknowledge the happiness currently existing in your life. You don't need to wait years to discover happiness. It is pretty much there; you just need to discover it. Being mindful makes you recognize that you are alive and breathing. It is when you are at harmony with the current moment as it comes. It might not be what you counted on or desired, but you are satisfied with it.

This is possibly among the most crucial habits you'll require to instill in your life if you intend to make it more Zen. Since it enables you to be comfortable with who you are and what you possess, it can easily be the happiest, most positive and the best spot to be. Additionally, being mindful offers you hope that you can accomplish a great deal more with life. Without a doubt it is the one option that'll empower you to appreciate life to the fullest. The easy trick hinges on not overlooking why something is essential, and doing it purposely.

The majority of people have their minds caught somewhere else. They just go through the day without really living it. This state is referred to as forgetfulness. Individuals stuck in this state can't cultivate concentration or remain in the present. They are either occupied remembering the past or stuck in the future.

Mindfulness is the precise opposite of forgetfulness. Mindfulness implies being there and residing in the present. A mindful state is one in which you are mentally engaged. Your mind and the body are each in one spot and this enables you to acknowledge joy around you and experience it.

Being mindful doesn't call for you to have particular powers to remain awake. All that you need to carry out is discover happiness in the little things. Here's just how you can discover to be a tad more mindful.

Slow Down

Running into things isn't often the ideal option. Planning the future and organizing tasks is a good idea but sometimes you need to do is to slow down. Things won't constantly go as intended; there will be area for improvements. Much like a lot of others, you may likewise be engrossed with speed. You wish to be faster, more efficient and more productive. To summarize, you just wish to be faster. Sidesteping the habit of hurrying and cramming things together might be especially tough if you wish to step in the Zen zone.

This is due to the fact that society rewards speed by means of career promotions, approval from peers and your impression that you're doing truly well. Yet, regardless of all the running around, you don't truly seem to be achieving anything additional. If anything, you get yourself more knotted into extra duties, paying less and less focus to each.

And to top it all, hastening around doesn't enable you to execute any better. Rather, it will raise your stress levels and make you more unpleasant. So take a minute and decelerate. You'll discover that you appreciate life more. Things will appear more fascinating and you'll have less to stress over.

Appreciate the Moment

Not everybody has the capability to appreciate moments, especially when you don't get what you anticipate. Say, you get stuck in a rush hour, the price of gas goes through the roof, or you get an upset look from someone. All these experiences are unsettling and some worrisome at best. So what do you do?

Presumably, you match up the present moment with what you expect to take place. A rush-hour will get you late to work. The cost of gas will unhinge your budget and you might spend the remainder of your day questioning what you did inappropriately to deserve that upset look.

In some cases, you need to give yourself space to breathe. Why muddle your life by concentrating on things that don't make a difference or are outside your control?

Instead, you can alleviate your life by appreciating what works out. There are a lot of things in life that can deliver joy. All that is needed on your behalf is the initiative. A lot of us also skip out on life's valuable moments simply as a result of stress. Life is uncertain, which is why it is essential to enjoy while you can.

For example, you can find happiness in the small things by understanding how to go with the flow. Sometimes life subjects you to surprises that can be positive or negative. To handle these curveballs you need to go with the flow. Going with the flow will allow you to take part in the actuality of life.

It's a Zen strategy that allows you to deal with what arrives your way and you make a decision based upon that. Simultaneously, it also means recognizing that good and bad things transpire in life and whenever they're outside your control, you acknowledge them as they come. This way, you allow yourself to take advantage of the moment regardless of any troubles.

Another way of considering this is that it allows you to surpass your failings. Acknowledging that you had a misstep means that you encounter the reality of the circumstance. And based upon that reality, you choose to proceed.

If you never acknowledge that truth, you'll get stuck at that moment. You'll probably proceed without veering, and after that, the past will catch up with you once more. You'll get entangled in the coil of past disappointments and be in no position to appreciate the moment.

Have Fewer Expectations

Expectations can cause dissatisfaction if things don't go in the direction you wish them to. Thus, expectations can be incredibly harmful to your joy and place your happiness on hold. Not to claim that you shouldn't have hopes. It's just that you ought to have less requirements if you intend to be happy.

That said, having reasonable expectations allows you to accept the imperfections in people. But having outlandish expectations will usually lead to dissatisfaction.

You might have expectations from other folks in addition to yourself. For example, you may anticipate that when you exercise and eat properly, you'll get that perfect body. Or once you put in the additional hours, you'll obtain that promotion. But when things don't turn out as you anticipated, you become aggravated, dissatisfied and mad with yourself and others.

Having less expectations allows you to acknowledge reality as it is. It also shows you that your life can continue to be great without many expectations. It is a humbling lesson that your life could be great as it is without counting on it to get better.

Having fewer expectations will prevent you from swaying back and forth based upon whether positive or negative things happen to you. Rather, you will no more expect positive or negative things to take place but just accept them as they arrive. This implies more contention for you and less dissatisfaction.

Whenever you cease judging things as desirable or negative, you'll feel less heavy and have more freedom.

Chapter 6: Don't Forget to Meditate Each Day

Meditation is an indispensable part of Zen habits. It is a long-established method that serves to help you soothe your mind, loosen up your body and focuses on comfort and stress alleviation. At its deepest level, meditation fulfills a spiritual purpose. Zen meditation centralizes around a kind of seated meditation referred to as zazen.

The practice is all about sitting straight and observing the breath. Other kinds of meditation work around concepts of mental focus on something. Still, others think that meditation consists of imagining a thing that offers you peace or pleasure. In either situation, the objective is to slow things down, particularly the mind and halt its constant activity.

Although Zen monks have understood it for years, now science also supports meditation as one of the most helpful ways of handling tension. Even though there are other stress-reduction procedures present, this one, without a doubt, is the most helpful.

You can meditate for a lot of various reasons. You can do so to cultivate focus, clarity, or even mental positivity. Depending on the kind of meditation technique you comply with, you can even discover the habits and patterns of your mind.

Most meditative states have a couple of fundamental commons. For example, to go into a state of meditation, you will have to assume an enjoyable posture.

Select a position that makes you feel pleasant but not too relaxed for you want to exercise your focus. You can meditate sitting, standing, kneeling or even lying down. Particular kinds of meditation will likewise allow you to sit in a chair and practice meditation.

Select a posture that normally comes to you. The trick is to maintain your spine straight. Going into a meditative state requires a few minutes. As you accomplish this, keep your eyes shut and keep track of your breathing. Breathing in and out eliminates diversions and reduces the heart rate.

Although there are many kinds of meditation, the emphasis here is on the primary three types, which are Yoga, Qigong, and Guided Visualization. Let's explore at each of these thoroughly.

Yoga

Yoga is a preferred meditation method that is performed widely and is also thought about as a popular kind of delicate exercises. Aside from helping acquire flexibility, strength, symmetry and even dropping weight, yoga provides tranquility to the mind.

Most yoga positions call for intense focus which itself has a soothing impact on the mind. This concentration also helps decrease stress as your mind focuses on your posture and nothing else. As you keep your posture, you also find out how to control your breath which has a soothing impact on the body and mind.

Even though yoga isn't a comprehensive cure for each ailment, it can be good for the human body in numerous ways. Yoga is the more cost effective treatment for a superior and healthier life. Some of the tangible benefits of Yoga entail:

Improved endurance

Enhanced flexibility

Improved balance

Improved strength

The psychological benefits that yoga delivers include:

Improved sleep

Decreased stress

Body awareness

Improved mindset

On a spiritual level, yoga strives to enable you to attain a total state of being. Sophisticated yogis can cultivate an internal toughness that provides total control over their emotions and wishes. On the inside, it allows them to withstand urges and worldly pleasures.

If you achieve an advanced level, you may likewise have the ability to find out how to boost your self-esteem by engaging in yoga. Removed from the concerns of the world, yogis can take in the truth better and begin to value themselves more.

Qigong

The second kind of meditation method is Qigong. This method serves to help strengthen posture and enables you to unwind with ease. It is one of the earliest types of meditation performed by the Chinese.

Qigong is composed of inner and outer movements. This technique mainly consists of the use of breath to move energy across the body. There are a couple of various styles classified as moving, still and sitting meditation.

Moving meditation with Qigong entails the change of energy through poses, movements, breathing habits and shifts. Postures that are maintained for extended periods of time fall under still meditation while sitting meditation concentrates more on the breathing, mind and body.

The movement that is performed in Qigong promotes organic energy. One division of Qigong referred to as medical Qigong is part of Conventional Chinese Medicine. It's utilized to advance self-healing, illness prevention and deals with illnesses.

The second, referred to as martial Qigong highlights physical skill. This kind allows practitioners to display physical accomplishments like smashing bricks and bending steel wires. The third style referred to as spiritual Qigong utilizes meditation techniques and prayers to go after enlightenment.

Whenever you utilize it for introspective purposes, Qigong can allow your body to develop a relationship with the spirit and mind. The technique allows you to establish deeper spiritual growth, body assurance and focus.

Yoga and Qigong are comparable in numerous ways as both contribute towards enhanced psychological health

.

Guided Visualization

Guided visualization is a kind of relaxation method that consists of creating an image of a calm environment in mind. This method is typically performed in isolation as it needs a fair bit of focus and attention. You are encouraged to develop a comprehensive mental image of a peaceful and eye-catching setting. The serene visual image is utilized to associate with the feeling of comfort to soothe the mind and body.

Guided visualization is also engaged in with physical methods like a massage or progressive muscle relaxation. The goal is to ensure that the mind goes into a state of calmness. The imagery utilized is used as a diversion tool to keep the mind away from things that may be straining you. You might obtain verbal or non-verbal guidelines to allow your mind to relax.

Engaging in this technique calls for both focus and creativity. It can not be performed in loud environments as disruptions quickly put you off track and returning into your peaceful state will be a lot harder.

This technique plays a huge part in improving focus abilities as the concentration is what is needed. It also affects cognitive capabilities and boosts memory power.

Guided visualization will demand that you think better in the absence of a congested mind. The method will enhance your creativity and magnify peaceful thinking. When undesirable thoughts interrupt your thinking process, directed visualization can allow you to do away with them.

People look for this method due to the fact that it allows them to unwind. Discovering peace can be a tough thing but generating it on your own is simple.

With directed visualization, you can increase inner peace by structuring a peaceful environment. Meditation is the conclusive Zen habit to integrate in your day. It may seem challenging but once engaged in can turn your life around.

Chapter 7: You Need a Daily Routine

Having an everyday routine is discipline. And discipline is what Zen habits are all about.

Whenever you have an established routine to adhere to, you can get more things accomplished and in less time. Routine brings in structure to your day and grants it a more organized and still feeling.

As you go throughout your day, you understand precisely what to do and this clarifies your workday and private life. With a time slot assigned to various tasks, you can better handle your day without cramping it excessively. But possibly the greatest benefit of having structure is that it places you in charge. You choose what's essential and what needs focus.

To make things simpler, you can split up your routines into daily and weekly activities. If you manage to stick to these for a minimum of one month, they'll end up being lifetime habits.

It's not just planning your day-to-day and weekly duties that require attention, but likewise how you look after yourself throughout this time.

You also want to develop healthy habits as part of your routine so you can look after your mind and body if you want to stay on top of your planned schedules. How do you accomplish that? You focus on these elements of your daily life.

Eating Well

You understand that you need to eat healthy but do you also understand the right way to do it? This is the point where lots of people get lost as they're unsure how to apply this understanding into action. But there is an easy way of accomplishing this. You may wonder about what the link between an established routine and eating is. Your eating habits determine your lifestyle.

In case you eat clean and wholesome, you will have a greater life and enhanced health. Whenever you eat healthy, you can operate better and end up being more lively. Your starting point for eating properly ought to be meal preparation. You can't go anyplace without this measure.

This will offer you a pretty good idea of what you'll consume and what you'll need to keep away from. This step also entails shopping in advance so that you have all the things with you when you begin cooking. Moving on, you ought to create your meals around truly nutritious foods. Naturally, you can have some wiggle room for minor indulgences, but the root of your eating plan ought to be founded on very healthy things.

Make it a habit to incorporate foods that you truly enjoy. This is extremely vital if you wish to eat properly for the remainder of your life. The reason why a lot of diets fall short is due to the fact that they focus on foods not everyone likes. If you can't/ don't consume what you enjoy, you won't stay with it for long. While anyone can comply with a restrictive diet for a couple of weeks at most, if you begin to feel starvation and anguish, you'll give it up in a short time.

So the trick to eating well continuously is to select healthy and enjoyable foods. You can also include multitude and mix up the plan from time to time. But the trick is to stick with the foods you enjoy. Another part is food preparation. Keep your recipes uncomplicated for you don't wish to be slaving over the stove forever. Select meals that are easy to put together and use less ingredients. By doing this, you'll save up on time in addition to cash.

Mind your portion size as you eat. In case you're eating proper, nutritious foods, then you won't need to go in for seconds and thirds. What you eat in one serving ought to be sufficient to last you till your following dish.

Exercise

When developing a daily routine, it is vital that you make physical exercise a component of your routine. Exercise not just keeps you in shape but likewise keeps you joyful and has a mind-calming impact. It can even work as therapy for certain people. Generally, people who work out tend to be more energetic and better-off than those who don't.

 But it may not be the most convenient habit to follow. Usually, people begin exercising with a great deal of energy and excitement. They tell themselves, they'll jog for 30 minutes each day or that they'll hit the gym every day. But the issue with this is that this kind of goal ends up being too difficult to sustain for long. You may manage to do it for a couple of days, but then you fatigue and the entire thing ends up being a drag.

You may likewise tell yourself that you'll exercise, eat well, give up desserts and go cold turkey on the soft drinks all at once. This strategy also produces issues because there are a lot of goals to handle simultaneously. Rather, what works in making physical exercise a routine part of your day is to begin simply. Keep your workout sessions quick and easy initially.

Decide on a time that'll work ideally for you. By doing this, you're more likely to go through and not put things off. Begin with a 15-20 minute session and persevere for a minimum of two weeks. As your body gets used to working out, you can then start extending your sessions and incorporating more intensity. But strive not to up the length and the intensity simultaneously.

As you work out, ensure that it's something you take pleasure in. As in the previous point, if you don't like what you eat, you'll quit healthy eating entirely. The same goes for physical activity. If you don't like what you do, you'll stop making it happen. Keep in mind that recovery is an integral part of the exercise.

You may not need to have a day of rest if you're only exercising casually for 20 minutes or so. But as you advance towards intermediate sessions, ensure to include rest days to give your body an opportunity to recover.

On your rest days, indulge in some very slight exercise like going out for a walk. The goal is to never really skip a day as this makes building a habit much harder. Do anything that keeps you in motion, even marginally. This will keep your habit creation moving.

Lower Stress

While a stress-free life is actually not achievable, you can try and reduce your stress levels significantly. It's achievable because a lot of the things you worry about are unwarranted. For the majority of people, stress comes from things such as meeting deadlines, handling difficult individuals, job unpredictability, competition, disputes, not enough time and a general sense of being overloaded by too much. Whenever things get out of control, you begin to freak out.

If you wish to reduce stress levels from your life, then you need to have some kind of a technique to accomplish so. For example, you need to acknowledge the indicators of stress. When you feel the stress showing up, pause and watch.

You may feel this as a bodily feeling of racing and crashing down. Or may acknowledge it as a headache starting. No matter what the signs, you need to stop and decelerate. If you sense that you're not in control any longer, just quit doing whatever is inducing this feeling. You need to acknowledge that you can't remain in control at all times, so don't let it overcome you.

Know that you can't accomplish everything at the same time, so pick your tasks carefully. Narrow your scope to bring things in context and renegotiate your obligations. Select only what is achievable and concentrate on one thing at a time. As you completely give yourself to that one thing, experience the pressure dissolve and relax into the moment.

Acknowledging what's happening will make you far better at reducing stress than attempting to fight it. If people give you stress, avoid them and remain with others who make you feel great. If things get in the way, separate yourself and meditate, stretch, massage or obtain some clean air until you are prepared to deal with the hurdles again.

Arrange to take mini breaks daily to destress on a regular basis. This is the sole way to recharge yourself for the following attack of the daily grind.

Chapter 8: Know How to Stop and Appreciate Life

People who manage to discover happiness in little things are those who live a cheerful life.

For others, it's effortless to overlook what they have since they're so occupied trying to find what they don't have. It's amusing how the mind functions, believing that what you could have will be more precious than what you do possess. But just how do you gauge this happiness?

There are individuals who have a bunch of money but aren't delighted and then there those who have no money but are joyful. This contrast occurs as a result of their mindset. Those who enjoy life find joy regardless of what.

While joy itself can imply a lot of various things for various individuals, those who are the happiest may not automatically have the finest of everything. But they do make the best of all things. If your joy is linked only with accomplishing certain goals like a lovely car or a decent job, then rest assured that the pursuit of joy will be a lifetime quest.

This is due to the fact that once you acquire these goals, you anticipate meeting additional goals which are going to make you happier and so forth. Simply put, your joy is always put somewhere down the road, but never in today.

On the other hand, happy people are regularly happy in the here and now. Their joy is right here and now with who they are and what they're undertaking. They find out to value life as it and don't give a thought to how excellent things are going to be in the years to come. If you wish to lead a better life, try incorporating these Zen habits to value life more.

Learn To Let Go

This might sound hard to accomplish, but learning to let go can release you from a great deal of concerns. Sometimes you stick on to things that don't make a difference. You think that if you release you won't manage to make it through.

Essentially, it's an effort to hang on to meaningless problems for more meaningful ones. When letting go, you want to understand that ignoring certain scenarios is a step forward. As a matter of fact, there are times when particular things in your life aren't meant to remain.

Maybe the most challenging part with regards to letting go is leaving your comfort zone and going into new areas. But keep in mind that change takes place for a reason and you ought to be prepared to welcome it.

Think about the example of a couple who separates. In either case, both parties included will be affected but until and unless they let go, they can't decrease the effect.

Gripping onto pain or nasty memories doesn't correct anything. If anything, it holds you back. It might be a tragedy, or an unforeseen death leaving you yearning for what might've been. You wish for what should've been or what you feel you were qualified for.

It might also be a desire, a wish, an expectation. Something that you might have desired for years but never realized.

It becomes very crucial to let go since all this is an impediment. And the longer you hold onto it, the longer it requires for you to proceed. The same also prevents you from investing in your today and enjoying the moment.

Even when you check out all the things you have, ask yourself- do you truly need to possess countless things?

That shirt you stopped putting on ages ago continues to hangs in your wardrobe. Those shoes that were your best friend in your university days still have a place on the shoe rack. You speak of letting go but keep holding onto excessive luggage. Learn to let go of stuff and allow more life in.

Turn More to Nature

There is no refuting the truth that everyone feels better when they are in nature. Mother Nature never lets us down and always offers inner calmness. Being in nature helps in reducing stress levels and if you observe, time likewise slows down when you find yourself in nature.

The feeling of urgency and hurry that you encounter in your everyday life appears to come to a standstill when you resort to nature. Rather, it's substituted by a healthier rate of life. Things in nature occur according to their natural cycle rather than being dictated by clock time.

When you spend more time in nature, you stop to appreciate the surroundings and discover how to value more. You learn to take a breath slowly and to loosen up and get alleviation from the grind. It is potentially among the best ways to incorporate more Zen into your life.

When you remove yourself from nature, you get absorbed by the drive to be as relaxed as attainable, to make your life as pleasant as achievable and to withstand as much hardship as you can. But the reality is that you can never be relaxed all the time. And you surely can't constantly be in control.

Remaining in contact with nature carries you back to reality. A lot of things in nature are outside your control like the ascending and setting sun. You can't govern when it rains or when the temperature gets too high. You discover how to acknowledge these components as they are, which is a lesson in humbleness. It makes you recognize how little control you actually have. You approve this truth and find out how to be content in your given situation.

Happiness Is Closer Than You Think

To wrap up, the pursuit of happiness doesn't need to be an inconceivable task. It's right there for you to witness if you select to do so.

As opposed to public opinion, which searches for the joy in better things, you can discover happiness in the most basic things. Have a successful day, engage in a walk in nature, or listen to a lovely tune. Discover how all these unimpressive things can make you happy. All you have to accomplish is to get in touch with joy, and it'll be right there for you.

Happiness isn't a thing that you can receive from outside things but stems from inside you. It is also not anything that occurs to you but something that you accomplish. And keep in mind that you'll never locate happiness if you keep searching in the wrong places.

To search for happiness externally prevents you from being yourself. So rather than looking for joy, just be yourself and you'll discover that joy will come to you.

Some people encounter a feeling of happiness through providing. This is due to the fact that providing connects you with others. So in case that's how you experience happiness, then donate generously.

You may likewise have reminisced over the past considering those "happier times." But if you concentrate enough and try to recall why you were delighted during the time that you presently think about as a happier time? You'll likely recognize that you never noted your joy as you encountered it. This is due to the fact that in your mind, happiness is a thing that resides in the memory as opposed to something you knowingly take in. To associate joy with either the past or the future leaves no space for it in the here and now.

This is what you need to alter. Concentrate on thankfulness and count your blessings so you can discover how to be happy in the now. Odds are you currently have joy in your midst but just don't recognize it.

Conclusion

A Zen lifestyle implies you need to filter, remove and edit a bunch of habits, belongings, attitudes and viewpoints from your life. All this is to streamline and minimize your life to render it a more deliberate existence.

It is a battle against velocity and time, where you get yourself out of the continuous surge of unending concerns and thoughts. You slow down the rate of your day-to-day life, get rid of everything that isn't necessary and appreciate life as it arrives your way. Try out these Zen habits and see how far better you'll feel with yourself.

I hope that you enjoyed reading through this book and that you found it useful. If you want to share your thoughts about this book, you can do so by leaving a review on the Amazon page. Have a great rest of the day.

Printed in Great Britain
by Amazon